Débora Samara Cruz Rocha Farias
Soahd A. R. Farias
José Dantas Neto

Groundwater quality for animal watering

Débora Samara Cruz Rocha Farias
Soahd A. R. Farias
José Dantas Neto

Groundwater quality for animal watering

Water stored in fissures in crystalline rocks

ScienciaScripts

Imprint

Cover image: www.ingimage.com

This book is a translation from the original published under ISBN 978-3-330-77274-8.

Publisher:
Sciencia Scripts
is a trademark of
Dodo Books Indian Ocean Ltd. and OmniScriptum S.R.L publishing group

120 High Road, East Finchley, London, N2 9ED, United Kingdom
Str. Armeneasca 28/1, office 1, Chisinau MD-2012, Republic of Moldova, Europe
Managing Directors: Ieva Konstantinova, Victoria Ursu
info@omniscriptum.com

Printed at: see last page
ISBN: 978-620-8-64337-9

SUMMARY

SUMMARY

This study assessed the quality of groundwater found in crystalline rock fissures for animal consumption from December 2014 to May 2015, located in the semi-arid region of Paraíba in the municipality of Boa Vista. 162 water samples were collected from different artesian wells in the region and taken for laboratory analysis. The field of study was the municipality of Boa Vista - PB, covering an area of 446.30 km^2 located at 7° 10' 11.5" and 7°22'1.6" South latitude and 36° 04' 19" and 36° 19' 17" West longitude. The region's climate, according to the Koppen classification, is of the BSh type, which means hot semi-arid, with an average rainfall of 416 mm/year. The research began in October 2014 and lasted until August 2015. Water samples were collected systematically in two stages in order to obtain the average salt content of the tube wells surveyed; in the first stage, 86 samples were collected from sources throughout the municipality, making a diagnosis of the quality of underground water; in the second stage, 76 water samples were collected, but this was reduced as some wells had dried up and others were broken; finally, the 76 wells were georeferenced. The points were georeferenced using a GPS 12 XL and photographed with a digital camera. The water was collected at the point where the water flowed, avoiding as far as possible contaminated reservoirs (drinking fountains) obtained directly from pumping. The salt contents were analyzed at the Irrigation and Salinity Laboratory (UFCG) by reading the water's electrical conductivity (ECa), determining the 4 cation and 3 anion salts, hydrogen potential (pH) and for the other parameters, formulas were used to obtain the alkalinity, total dissolved salts (STD) and hardness of the water from the municipality of Boa Vista, PB. Most of the pH values are within the normal range for animal consumption. For birds, which are more sensitive, a reasonable percentage of samples were found to be outside the drinking water standards, representing a possible risk to the health of birds in the area studied. The electrical conductivity of the region is quite high, unsuitable for animals; in both samples the chloride values were well above those recommended for animal consumption. technical recommendation is to build cisterns to dilute the water with high conductivity that will be offered to the animals, irrigation with saline water should be done for tolerant crops and the implantation of tanks for raising tilapia and shrimp.

Keywords: water quality, classification, salinity.

1 INTRODUCTION

The Boa Vista-PB region is located in the semi-arid northeastern region of Brazil and its groundwater contains a large amount of salts, which can affect poultry performance. Brazilian poultry farming has established itself as one of the most important and efficient agricultural activities, with high growth rates. Brazil is the third largest producer in the world and the leading exporter, thanks to constant and significant investments in modernizing poultry houses, ambience, health, nutrition and proper management (BRASIL, 2013).

The scarcity of drinking water is causing great concern in society, mainly because without it, life is unviable. Like all livestock, poultry farming is highly dependent on water, so when planning poultry farming, one must be aware of the importance of this resource for the activity and take care to manage it, so that it does not become a quantitative or qualitative limiting factor, as well as a cause for conflict with the community (PALHARES, 2011). In industrial poultry farming, water must be available in adequate quantity and quality to serve all sectors of the production chain (OLIVEIRA, 2010).

In poultry farming, water should be given the same importance as other factors such as facilities, feed and management. Production birds need a large amount of water for their development and well-being (SOARES, 2010). Poultry farming can affect water resources in a number of ways, from the incorrect management of drinking troughs, resulting in excessive water consumption, to the application of waste to the soil with potential risks of pollution and contamination of groundwater and surface water (PALHARES, 2011).

The main sources of water for poultry farms are groundwater and surface water (MACARI & SOARES, 2012). Water is the most important nutrient consumed by poultry (VIOLA et al., 2011). Several essential functions of the animal organism are directly related to water, such as digestion of food; absorption of nutrients in the digestive tract; translocation of chemical compounds in the body; secretion of hormones, enzymes and other biochemical substances; body thermoregulation;

maintenance of osmotic pressure inside and outside the cell; acid-base balance; constitutes the majority of cerebrospinal, synovial, auricular and intraocular fluid (LIMA and PIOCZCOVSKI, 2010).

According to VIOLA et al., (2011) when the salinity of the water increases, the birds increase their water consumption until the moment when they refuse to consume duc to excess salinity, in extreme cases, when the minerals that are in excess in the water are known, they can be totally or partially removed from the formulation of the diets.

According to the Companhia de Desenvolvimento dos Recursos Minerais da Paraiba (CDRM), in 2011 the agency drilled and installed 310 wells; in 2012 there were 195; in 2013 there were 395 and the total reached 685 wells in 2014 throughout Paraiba. Even in the crystalline semi-arid northeastern region of Brazil, where the productivity of wells is very low (usually less than 3 m^3/h) and the water is highly saline, in many small communities these wells are the only available source of supply (PNRH, 2006).

The region of Boa Vista - PB is located in the northeastern semi-arid region and has had a great deal of government incentive, as well as bank financing and producers' own resources for drilling wells in the last 5 years (2012 to August 2016), due to a high reduction in annual rainfall in those years (2012-2014), thus trying to achieve the purpose of maintaining livestock activities, including, Cattle with 5800 head, sheep with 4600 head, pigs with 500 head, goats with 6800 head, horses with 180 head, quails with 1300 head and chickens with 19000 head (IBGE, 2014), many underground wells were demanded for the region, without observing the physical-chemical quality as a means of drilling criteria, especially for poultry, which is among the group most sensitive to salt levels.

The aim of this study was to evaluate the quality of groundwater used for animal watering in the Boa Vista-PB region, by analyzing the physical and chemical parameters.

2. MATERIAL AND METHODS

The field of study was the municipality of Boa Vista, covering an area of 446.30 km^2, located between latitudes 7°09'03.7" and 7°22'19.7" south latitude and 36°05'25.6" and 36°22'22.8" west longitude. The region's climate, according to the Koppen classification, is of the BSh' type, which means hot semi-arid, with an average rainfall of 416 mm/year (AESA, 2016).

The Boa Vista region is part of crystalline aquifers under crystalline rocks. These rocks have a reduced capacity to store and circulate their groundwater, and often have an excessive concentration of salts, especially where the conditions for recharge from rainfall are poorer, presenting water with a higher degree of mineralization (ROCHA, 2008).

Groundwater is a resource resulting from a process in which the climate and its elements interact with the physiography of the state, and is also influenced by its geological composition (PARAIBA, 1994). It should be noted that the municipality is not in a position to form large springs due to the adverse climatic conditions and unfavorable physiography, with shallow soils that favor surface runoff, sparse and small vegetation cover and rock formations with low permeability, such as igneous and metamorphic rocks, which limits the possibility of infiltration and possible underground water storage through fractures, with the crystalline as the only aquifer system (FALCÂO, 2013).

Some of the main plant species that occur in the municipality of Boa Vista-PB are: umbuzeiro (*Spondias tuberosa*), angico (*Anadenanthera colubrina var. cebil (Griseb.*), juazeiro (*Ziziphus joazeiro* Mart.), catingueira (*Caesalpinia pyramidalis* Tul.), pereiro (*Aspidosperma pyrifolium* Mart.), marmeleiro (Croton sonderianus Muell. Arg.), quixabeira (*Bumelia sertorium* Mart.), aroeira (*Myracrodruon urundeuva* Allemào), braùna (*Schinopsis brasiliensis* Engl.), juremapreta (*Mimosa tenuiflora*), xique-xique (*Pilosocereus gounellei* Weber), macambira (*Bromelia laciniosa* Mart. ex Schult.f.) and mandacaru (*Cereus jamacaru* DC.) (NASCIMENTO e OLIVEIRA, 2005; AGRA et al., 2007).

According to AESA (2016), the municipality of Boa Vista, located in the state of Paraiba, has climatological annual rainfall expectations of less than 500 mm per year. During the research, the municipality received water well below what is considered average (climatology) for the location.

Checking the distribution of accumulated rainfall over the months of each year, it can be seen in this municipality that there are characteristics of high temporal variation between the months of January to December, in addition to representing small and non-regular values, and even the month considered to have the highest rainfall (March) sees practically no rain at all (years 2010, 2012, 2013), 2012, 2013), which makes it impossible to grow most annual crops, which require an average of 300 to 500 mm in a cycle of 3 to 5 months, so the expected climatology is not sufficient for planning any rainfed farming. According to Table 1, the months from August to December are marked by low or almost no rainfall, a very short period of rain and/or irregular distribution throughout the year.

Table 1. Distribution of accumulated monthly rainfall between 2014 and 2015 in the municipality of Boa Vista - PB.

Precipitation (mm)	**Jan**	**Feb**	**Sea**	**Apr**	**May**	**Jun**	**Jul**	**Aug**	**Set**	**Out**	**Nov**	**Ten**
Year 2015	0,0	5,8	3,4	0,0	9,1	21,1	70,9	5,4	0,0	0,0	0,0	12,8
Year 2014	0,0	38,9	11,0	48,6	117,2	30,4	37,6	5,2	31,0	17,9	13,8	0,0
Climatology	26,0	35,2	82,3	69,4	58,7	53,0	45,9	19,2	5,5	6,6	4,3	9,4

Source: AESA (2016)

Associated with a very low expectation of rainfall are shallow soils, predominantly non-calcareous Bruno soils in the region, mostly composed of solodic Planossolo (Solodized Soloncтez), which has a great influence on the release of salts during the rainy season, leaving the streams with brackish and saline water, as well as some patches of Eutrophic Litholic (Figure 1); According to EMBRAPA (2016), these conditions are more limiting in terms of the use and agricultural exploitation capacity of the soil, requiring awareness in relation to its productive exploitation.

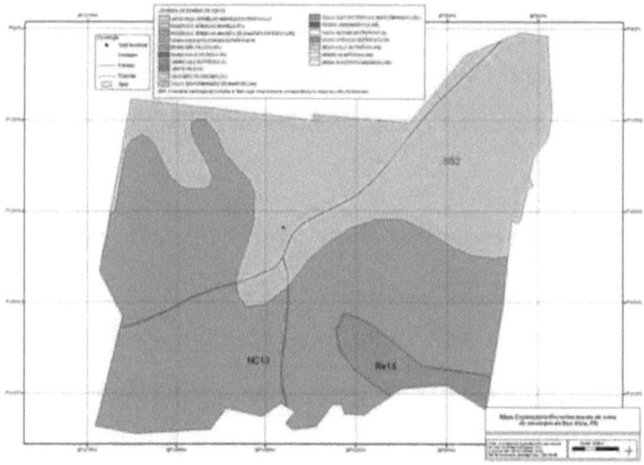

Figure 1. Predominant characteristics of existing soil types in the region of the municipality of Boa Vista - PB. **Source:** EMBRAPA (2016).

According to AESA (2016), there are three classes of land use capacity, with a higher proportion of uncultivated land with severe limitations, steep land more susceptible to erosion, suitable for continuous cultivation and more suitable for sporadic farming; there is also stony land, severely eroded, sandy and waterlogged, suitable for sheltering wildlife and preserving natural flora. It is imperative that care is taken to conserve agricultural soils, since this is linked to the prosperity of being able to infiltrate more water during the rains, make more nutrients available and, consequently, guarantee production even in situations of longer rainfall intervals, since the soils in this region are shallow and young and, furthermore, have problems with salt levels in their water, both surface and underground, requiring greater knowledge of the potential of these sources for the rural community to have greater security in their use.

Analyzing Figure 2 in terms of land use capacity, it can be seen that the purple color in the legend indicates "*Lands with stony soil, severely eroded, sandy and waterlogged, suitable for sheltering wild fauna and preserving natural flora*", for white patches "*Ingrained land more susceptible to erosion, suitable for continuous cultivation and more suitable for sporadic farming*" *and* for brown patches "*Uncultivated land with severe limitations for permanent crops and reforestation*".

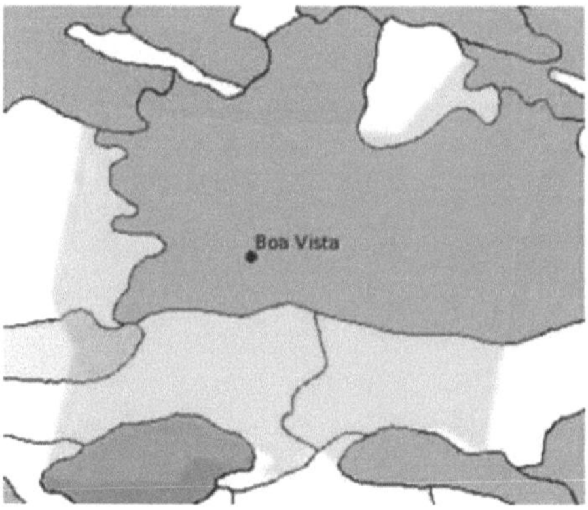

Figure 2. Land use capacity characteristics for the region of the municipality of Boa Vista - PB. **Source:** AESA (2016).

The research was carried out in the region of the municipality of Boa Vista-PB, in the communities of Malhadinha, Bravo, Roçado do Mato, Lajes, Rabicha, Mônica in the semi-arid region of the Northeast. 162 water samples were collected from underground wells.

2.1 CONDUCTING FIELDWORK

The research began in October 2014 and lasted until August 2015, when it was repeated in two stages to obtain the maximum, minimum, average and median values of the salt content of the tube wells surveyed.

2.2 DATA COLLECTION PROCEDURES

In the first stage, 86 samples were collected from sources throughout the municipality, and a diagnosis was made of the quality of its groundwater.

With regard to the second stage, only 76 samples were collected from sources throughout the municipality, as some wells had broken or dried up, and a diagnosis was made of the quality of their groundwater. The points were georeferenced using a GPS 12 XL (Figure 3) and photographed with a digital camera.

Figure 3: Georeferenced points used in Google Earth, 2016

2.3 WATER SAMPLE COLLECTION PROCEDURE

To collect the water, 2-liter plastic bottles were used, which were washed with water from the tube well to be analyzed; the bottles were quickly immersed with their mouths down to a depth of 15 to 30 cm below the surface of the water and then tilted, directing their mouths upwards (preferably collection directly from pipes Figure 2, pumped by a wind vane and in closed reservoirs to prevent the water from being contaminated from the outside or evaporating, producing a concentration of salts unrealistic to the condition of the well). The water was also collected in closed tanks (Figure 3). After the bottles were filled to the brim, leaving no empty space (air bubbles), they were closed immediately with their own caps, so as not to leave any leaks.

Figure 4: Collecting water samples directly from the tube

Figure 5: Collection of water samples in a closed reservoir

After the collection procedure, the bottles were identified and brought to UFCG's Irrigation and Salinity Laboratory (Figure 6). Particular information about each well was recorded on a field form, such as: owner's name, property, altitude, latitude, longitude, type of pumping source and its main uses.

Figure 6. Waters analyzed at the UFCG Irrigation and Salinity Laboratory.

2.4 TYPES OF SOURCE

Figure 7 shows all the types of collection sources in the municipality from which water samples were taken. The largest number of water samples in the municipality were collected from a wind vane (45), Figure 7A, followed by an electric pump (28), Figure 7B, and a compressor (3), Figure 7C. Another 10 samples could not be collected because the wells were dry or broken.

Figure 6 - Water sample collection sites, wind vane (A), electric pump (B) and compressor (C)

During the collections, a field form was drawn up which included the date, general registration number, information on where the water sample was collected, the owner's name, latitude, longitude, altitude, type of source and main purposes. The water analysis was carried out at the Irrigation and Drainage Laboratory, part of the UAEA/UFCG, in the city of Campina Grande, PB. The irrigation water quality parameters analyzed were: pH, magnesium, SDT, hardness, potassium, calcium and sodium. The samples were collected in 2014 and 2015.

Table 2 shows examples of the water potability standards established for poultry watering, in which it can be seen that some of the parameters required for poultry are very similar to human standards, in some cases the levels for poultry are even more restrictive.

Salinity ($dS\ m^{-1}$)	**Class**	**Remarks**
< 1,5	Excellent	Suitable for all classes
1,5 - 5,0	Very satisfactory	Causes diarrhea in unaccustomed cattle and watery droppings in birds
5,0 - 8,0	Satisfactory for livestock; Not satisfactory for poultry	May produce temporary diarrhea or be unacceptable to unaccustomed animals

		Increased mortality and reduced growth, especially in turkeys
8,0 - 11,0	Limited use for livestock; Not suitable for poultry	Avoid for pregnant and lactating females Not suitable for poultry
11,0 - 16,0	Limited use	High risk for lactating or pregnant cows. Older animals can survive under certain conditions
>16,0	Not recommended	Very big risks.

Table 3 shows the tolerable levels of magnesium according to the Australian Water Resources Council (1969) cited by Ayers and Westcot (1999).

Table 3. Suggested levels of magnesium in drinking water (cattle and poultry[1)].

Poultry and Cattle	**Magnesium concentration**	
	mg L^{-1}	**meq L^{-1}**
Confined poultry[2]	< 250	< 21
Pigs[2]	< 250	< 21
Horses	< 250	< 21
Lactating cows	< 250	< 21
Sheep and lambs	< 250	< 21
Beef cattle	< 400	< 33
Adult sheep fed hay	< 500	< 41

[1]**Source**: Australian Water Resources Council (1969), quoted by AYERS and WESTCOT (1999).

[2] The tolerance of poultry and pigs to Mg is unknown; it is estimated to be less than 250 mg L^{-1}.

Table 4- Water quality standards for poultry watering.

Elements or contaminants	**Average level considered (mg L-1)**	**Maximum acceptable level (mg L-1)**
pH	6,8 - 7,5	-
Hardness	60 - 180	-
Calcium	60	-

Chloride	14	250
Magnesium	14	125[1]
Sodium	32	-

For animal consumption, as cited by Ayers and Westcot (1999), the US National Academy of Sciences classifies water by recommending salinity parameters between 1.5 and 16 (dS m^{-1}), as shown in Table 4.

According to Ayers and Westcot (1999), with the exception of magnesium, most of the ions responsible for salinity are not very toxic. Thus, Australian standards recommend that Mg should be considered, especially when salinity exceeds 6600 uS m^{-1} (4,000 mg L^{-1}) in water for cattle and 10000 uS m^{-1} (6,000 mg $L^{(-1)}$) in water for sheep. Table 4 shows the tolerable levels of magnesium Australian Water Resources Council (1969) cited by Ayers and Westcot (1999).

Table 5. Classification of water for animal consumption (cattle and poultry).

Animal species/category	**Acceptable chloride content (mg L^{-1} of Cl)**
Dairy cattle	1600
Beef cattle	4000
Sheep and lambs	2400
Adult sheep	5600
Equidae (horses)	1200

Maximum chloride levels for some animal species/categories (Adapted from "Water for livestock: interpreting water quality tests")

3. RESULTS AND DISCUSSION

3.1 ELECTRICAL CONDUCTIVITY OF WATER (CEA)

The ECa of the water samples ranged from 0.69 to 17.904 dS m^{-1}, with a mean of 7.2624 and a median of 7.190 with a standard deviation of 3734.5 (1st collection), and a minimum of 1143.0 to 17.904 dS m^{-1}, with a mean of 7.8415 and a median of 7.5705 with a standard deviation of 3834.4 (2nd collection). The electrical conductivity values were very high, indicating a longer residence time for these waters and, conversely, a greater tendency to salinization. This characteristic is attributed to the way in which the water percolates through the rock, in a discontinuous way and with slow circulation, leading to greater interaction between the water and the rock present in crystalline aquifers (ROCHA, 2008).

These are mostly salty waters, and it is worrying that these underground waters are withdrawn without any criteria; they are spread on the surface of the soil and in the diet of animals, increasing the levels of salts on the surface, these salts crystallize when the rains occur, they are carried to the springs and the tendency is for the surface waters to become increasingly salty. The water from these tube wells is often poorly conveyed, overflowing into the water tanks (Figures 8 and 9), somehow adding up these salts within the basin, a place that has already suffered from brackish surface water, as seen in previous research in 2013 and 2014, which could concentrate more salts in the reservoirs and have the Epitàcio Pessoa (Boqueirao) reservoir as its next and worrying destination.

Figure 8. Water overflowing from the water tank.

Figure 9. Water being wasted from the animal drinking trough.

During the research period, the ECa values of the water from the various tube wells remained high, which is confirmed by hydrochemical studies of underground springs in the northeast region (IBGE, 2013); the region has poor to non-potable quality on maps of the region, and it is important to find, through such a study, isolated sources that may offer some difference from what has generally been found in previous studies. The mineral origin of the rock and a low rainfall regime contribute greatly to remaining high and impossible to use for human consumption.

The variation in salt levels in the tube wells is perceived as small since they are replenished by the infiltration of rainwater into the soil and fractures. From 2012 to 2015, according to AESA (2016) rainfall data, the average rainfall over the last four years was around 213.6 mm, i.e. without significant annual rainfall, the variation in salts found in the tube wells in the two stages was small.

According to Molle and Cadier (1992), the concentration of salts in water is perceptible to the palate when the ECa reaches values above 0.8 dS m^{-1}. Taking into account this value and the EC results of the water samples from Boa Vista - PB, it can be said that 98.68% would have a salty taste, which would be unpleasant for humans. Sawyer and McCarty (1987) state that many populations around the world consume water with an EC of more than 0.8 dS m^ 1, without harming their health.

3.2 ANALYSIS OF DESCRIPTIVE STATISTICS

The descriptive statistics for all the water collected throughout the year from November 2014 to August 2015, Table 11, showed an average electrical conductivity of 7262.4 uS cm^{-1} at 25 °C and a high coefficient of variation of 51.4, which classifies it as unviable for animal watering. The coefficient of variation was very high because the values differ greatly from one source to another, they are not homogeneous sources.

According to the results in Table 6, with the exception of pH, there was a high degree of variation in the concentration of the other parameters studied (EC, Mg, Ca, Na, K, bicarbonate, chloride and carbonate); also, the coefficient of variation was very high for these parameters, indicating a high degree of variability in the quality of the water from the points sampled. The standard deviation shows a high dispersion around the mean, thus demonstrating the complexity and heterogeneity in the behavior of the water variables in the crystalline rock region as a whole. This suggests different conditions for recharge, storage and the dynamics of underground flow in the fissure environment. This great statistical variability attests to the need to establish hydrochemical zoning by region, with possible influences from the physiographic and climatic characteristics of each context (COSTA, 2006).

Table 6. Results of the main parameters determined in water samples collected from sources located in the state of Paraiba.

	Ph	**ECa (uS/cm)**	**Ca^{++} (mg L^{-1})**	**Mg^{++} (mg L^{-1})**	**In^{+} (mg L^{-1})**	**K^{+} (mg L^{-1})**	**$CO_3^{=}$ (mg L^{-1})**	**HCO_3^{-} (mg L^{-1})**	**Cl^{-} (mg L^{-1})**
Average	8,7	7262,4	194,6	259,4	1013,3	56,9	80,2	309,1	2437,3
Median	7,6	7190,0	141,6	237,1	920,0	24,6	57,6	301,6	2258,2
Standard deviation		3734,5	157,9	155,3	585,5	230,5	131,5	157,6	1520,0
Maximo	10,1	17550,0	632,2	803,0	3385,1	2152,0	1104,0	648,4	7768,1
Minimum	6,1	690,0	6,8	11,5	101,2	3,9	0,0	59,2	35,5
Coefficient of variation	334,2%	51,4%	81,1%	59,9%	57,8%	405,3%	163,8%	51,0%	62,4%

The descriptive statistics of the 2nd collection, all the waters, according to Table 7, had an average electrical conductivity of 7841.5 uS/cm at 25 °C, classified as not recommended for human consumption. High electrical conductivity is associated with excessive mineralization which manifests itself in the form of an unpleasant taste, unviable for animal watering. The ECa values have a coefficient of variation of 48.9. The coefficient of variation was very high for all the variables, because the values differed greatly from one source to another. Even the maximum value of 17.940 dS m^{-1} of electrical conductivity of the water can still be considered a low level of salinity for Atriplex nummularia, since this plant can produce good yields, even when irrigated with water of salinity levels equivalent to 57.0 dS m^{-1}, these plants can be offered to animals because they produce a good amount of fodder. (FAO, 1996).

Table 7. Results of the main parameters determined in water samples collected from sources located in the state of Paraiba.

	Ph	**ECa (uS/cm)**	**Ca^{++} (mg L^{-1})**	**Mg^{++} (mg L^{-1})**	**In^{+} (mg L^{-1})**	**K^{+} (mg L^{-1})**	**$CO_3^{=}$ (mg L^{-1})**	**HCO_3^{-} (mg L^{-1})**	**Cl^{-} (mg L^{-1})**
Average	8,24	7841,5	212,8	296,1	985,2	34,2	83,4	264,7	2770,1
Median	7,9	7190,0	141,6	237,1	920,0	24,6	57,6	301,6	2258,2
Deviation		3834,4	165,0	173,5	555,7	32,0	66,8	107,7	1561,2

standard									
Maximo	9,0	17904,0	711,0	691,4	3385,1	179,4	496,8	608,2	7091,1
Minimum	6,6	1143,0	26,0	33,0	101,2	3,1	0,0	56,1	146,3
Coefficient of variation	137,29 %	48,9%	77,5%	58,6%	56,4%	93,5%	80,1%	40,7%	56,4%

The amount of carbonates in the waters studied is much lower than that of bicarbonates. No pH values above 10 were found. Carbonate only exceeds bicarbonate when the pH is equal to or greater than 10 (LOGAN, 1965).

3.3 MAP OF THE ELECTRICAL CONDUCTIVITY OF WATER IN THE municipality of BOA VISTA - PB

Figure 10 was created using Surfer software, based on the latitude and longitude coordinates of the region and the electrical conductivity of the water at each point, which ranged from 0.690 dS m^{-1} in the Lajes community to 17.550 dS m^{-1} in the Sao Bento community. High conductivity values have a high correlation with salinity due to the nature of the more frequent fracturing and the smaller spacing of the openings, promoting greater interaction between the rock and the water (ROCHA, 2008).

This map shows the areas with the highest salt concentrations. Halophyte plants grow naturally in environments with high salt concentrations (typically Na^+ and Cl^-), which can vary from 4.5 to 14.0 dS m^{-1} (WILLADINO; CAMARA, 2005).

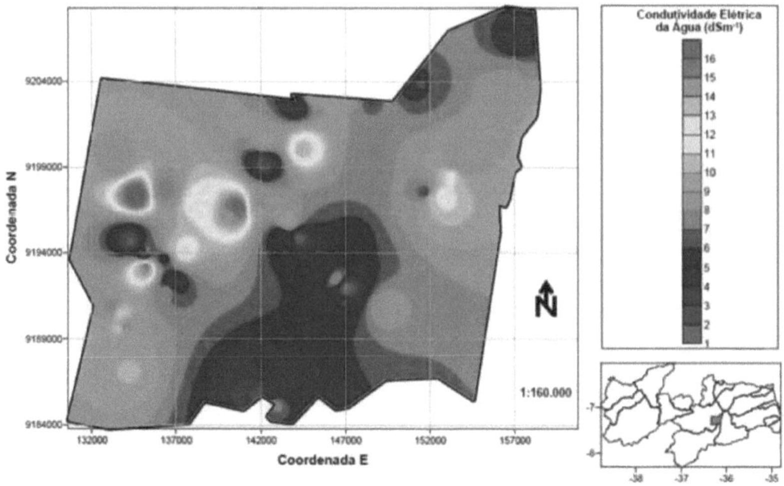

Figure 10. Electrical conductivity of water from the Boa Vista - PB region.

Comparing the map of the *water*'s electrical conductivity with the soil map drawn up by AESA (2016), we can see that the red spots are Solondez Solodizado soils, which have a great influence on the release of salts during the rainfall process, infiltrating and being incorporated into the groundwater, denoting a high value of the *water*'s electrical conductivity.

In the Malhadinha community, this source is fed by a compressor (Figure 11); the *water* was collected from a pipe that releases directly from the well. The water has an extremely high level of electrical conductivity (10.5 dS m^{-1}), which makes it unsuitable for human consumption, animal watering and irrigation, and it is only used for bathing pigs.

Figure 11. Water for bathing the pigs.

Figure 12. Water sampling in an open reservoir.

Mônica Community (Figure 12): this is a wind-powered fountain and its water was collected from an open reservoir with an extremely high level of electrical conductivity (14.3 dS m^{-1}). The entire reservoir was corroded by the salts present in the water.

3.4 WATER QUALITY FOR POULTRY

As the region has a significant poultry industry of around 223,000 head (IBGE, 2014), the water quality for the birds was analyzed.

According to Scheideler and Pendleton (1995), the pH should be between 6.8 and 7.5. Of the 86 water samples analyzed in the first collection, 40.70% were outside this limit and in the second collection 71.05%. The higher the pH of the water, the greater the need for chlorine as a disinfectant.

The pH of the water in Boa Vista ranges from 6.07 to 10.07 (1st collection) and 6.58 to 9.01 (2nd collection), which according to Scheideler and Pendleton (1995) can be considered unsatisfactory and not suitable for birds.

The results of the analysis of the poultry water samples showed 59.30% alkaline pH in the first collection and 75% in the second collection. Alkalinity is found in water in the form of carbonates and bicarbonates and results from the presence of weak acid salts, carbonates, bicarbonates, hydroxides and, occasionally, silicates and phosphates, and can be caustic (MACÊDO, 2004).

Viola et al. (2011) reported that birds did not decrease their consumption of water with a pH between 2.0 and 10.0. In addition, Gama et al. (2004) state that drinking water with an acidic pH can improve performance. For Pomiano (2002) and Gama et al. (2008) the consumption of water with a pH between 6.0 and 8.0 can alter bird performance, affect broiler performance, egg production and quality in layers, precipitate antibiotics and interfere with the efficiency of water chlorination, so there is disagreement on this issue.

Correcting the pH of the water is also important for administering medicines and vaccinations via drinking water, as extreme pH values impair the survival of vaccine viruses when diluted in water for mass application to birds, the dissolution of the antibiotic tylosin and promote the precipitation of sulphonamides (GAMA et al., 2004).

According to Vohra (1980), hardness is not harmful to birds, unless the ions are present in large quantities, which makes the water toxic and can increase mortality due to cardiovascular diseases in birds (NERI et al., 1975).

It has been speculated that hardness may be related to the onset of fatty liver syndrome in layers, although Jensen et al. (1977) were unsuccessful in demonstrating this relationship experimentally.

Pomiano (2002) also reports that water used in poultry farms should ideally have a hardness level of up to 60 mg L^{-1}, with levels of up to 110 mg L^{-1} of $CaCO_3$ being tolerated, with deleterious effects occurring after this level. According to Lagger et al. (2000), hardness can interfere with the microbiological quality of water, due to the lack of efficiency of detergents in sanitizing equipment, and this effect becomes important when it exceeds 100 mg L^{-1} of calcium carbonate. According to Macari (1996), the quality of water for poultry is very hard (above 180 mg L^{-1}), which represents 98.84% (1st collection) and 86.84% (2nd collection).

Among the minerals present in water hardness are calcium and magnesium. The biggest problem with water hardness is not related to its quality for animals, as few are directly affected by this factor. However, excess hardness can compromise the pipes by accumulating material in the system, impairing the flow of water in the troughs and thus indirectly harming the birds. Water with more than 180 ppm $CaCO_3$ is considered very hard and should be avoided. Water hardness influences the ability of soap and detergent to form foam, a characteristic that should also be observed in the water used on farms, interfering with the cleaning and disinfection of facilities. Water hardness refers mainly to the concentration of calcium and magnesium ions in solution, forming precipitates due to calcium and magnesium carbonates, and is expressed as mg L^{-1} of $CaCO_3$. High levels of hardness can lead to an unpleasant taste in the water, incrustations in the pipes, a laxative effect and interference in the efficiency of some medicines and disinfectants, such as quaternary ammonia, which is less effective (BLOCK, 1991; MOUCHREK, 2003; GAMA et al., 2004; FAIRCHILD and RITZ, 2006).

As previously reported, the presence of calcium is related to hardness, with 60 mg L^{-1} being the maximum acceptable level for poultry water. Of the samples analyzed, 17.44% (1st collection) and 21.05% (2nd collection) were within the range allowed for poultry. Calcium rarely causes intoxication problems in poultry and increasing its levels in water has been correlated with better feed conversion and body weight, but with reduced flock viability (ÀGUA, 1988).

The maximum concentration of potassium in chicken water has not yet been determined, but in drinking water for humans, it is classified as dissolved solids and its maximum amount is determined to be 10 mg L^{-1} of water (Vohra, 1980). Marks (1987) showed that an increase in potassium in the diet promotes an increase in water consumption by broiler chickens. During the evaluation of the water from the tube wells, the quality of the water for poultry as a function of the potassium content (10 mg L^{-1}) was 86.05% above the maximum permitted value in both samples.

According to the NRC (1974), values below 1,000 ppm of total dissolved salts are considered low for the use of water for poultry, making it possible to supply water to any species of poultry, and 1.16% of the water samples analyzed in the study were within this value. On the other hand, concentrations of total dissolved salts in water ranging from 1,000 to 2,999 ppm are considered satisfactory for supplying any species of poultry, but without harming their health or productive performance, they can cause wet droppings, which represents 12.79% of the samples analyzed.

On the other hand, concentrations of total dissolved salts in water ranging from 3,000 to 4,999 ppm are considered unsatisfactory for supplying to poultry, often causing wet droppings, increased mortality and decreased performance (turkeys), which represents 17.44% of the samples analyzed within this range.

Between 5,000 and 6,999 ppm of total dissolved salts in water is not acceptable for birds, it compromises growth and increases mortality, which represents 17.44%, within this range in both collection periods.

Between 7,000 and 10,000 ppm of total dissolved salts, the water cannot be used for birds, but it can be used for other types of animals, which represents 31.40% of the samples analyzed. Above 10,000 ppm it cannot be used for any species of animal, 19.77% of samples were above 10,000 in the first collection and 25% in the second collection.

The biggest problem with water hardness is not related to its quality for animals. They are hardly affected by this factor. However, excess hardness can severely compromise pipes due to the accumulation of material in the system. This compromise of the pipes can impair the flow of water in the troughs and thus indirectly harm the broilers. The chemical composition of the water affects the sanitary condition of the intestines and certain medicines may not solubilize in water that is too hard and has an inadequate pH. A chemical characteristic called Total Dissolved Solids (TDS) or Salinity gives us a good reference of the water's chemical quality.

The minerals that normally contribute most to TDS values are calcium, magnesium, sodium, chlorine, bicarbonate and sulphur (PENZ JÙNIOR, 2002; MACÊDO, 2007).

SDT analysis is an important parameter to monitor when it comes to water quality in poultry production, because as SDT increases, water quality worsens, causing a decrease in water consumption and losses in poultry performance (NRC, 1974).

Of the water from the tube wells analyzed, 96.51% of the water in the first collection and 97.37% in the second collection is not suitable for poultry in terms of chloride. High chloride levels can give the water a salty taste (MOUCHREK, 2003).

3.5 CLASSIFICATION OF WATER FOR ANIMAL CONSUMPTION

The chemical and physical parameters that define the quality limits of water for animal consumption are very varied, including pH, electrical conductivity of the water, magnesium, sodium, chloride, potassium and calcium. As far as water quality is concerned, in the sense that goats and sheep have the ability to withstand more salinized water than cattle, and cattle in relation to horses and pigs, while poultry may have a much lower level of tolerance to salinity, as they are much more sensitive animals.

Looking at Figure 13, a total of 5.81% (1st collection) and 2.63% (2nd collection) of the samples have electrical conductivity below 1500 uS/m, which is excellent quality water, suitable for all classes without any risk to any animal; 25.58% (1st collection) and 23.68% (2nd collection) have water with an electrical conductivity between 1500 and 5000 uS/m, which is water of very satisfactory quality that can cause diarrhea in unaccustomed cattle and watery droppings in birds; 29.07% (1st collection) and 27.63% (2nd collection) have water with an electrical conductivity between 5000 and 8000 uS/m that is satisfactory for cattle and unsatisfactory for birds; These waters can produce temporary diarrhea or be unacceptable to unaccustomed animals and increase mortality by reducing growth, especially in turkeys.

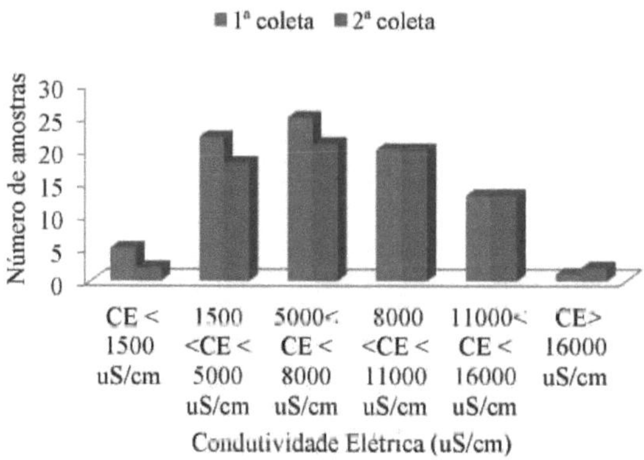

Figura 12. Electrical conductivity of water for animals

It was found that 23.26% (1ª collection) and 26.32% (2ª collection) of the water samples had an electrical conductivity of between 8000 and 11000 uS/m, and are therefore considered to be of limited use for livestock. This water is not suitable for consumption by poultry, especially pregnant and lactating females; Therefore, it is not suitable for poultry, 15.12% (1st collection) and 17.11% (2nd collection) of the water samples have an electrical conductivity between 11,000 and 16,000 uS/m of limited use causing great risks for lactating or pregnant cows and older animals can survive in certain conditions and 1,16% (1st collection) and 2.63% (2nd collection) have water with an electrical conductivity above 16000 uS/m, which is not recommended and poses very high risks according to the US National Academy of Sciences (1972) apud Ayers and Westcot (1999) for classifying water for animal consumption.

The ideal level for birds is an electrical conductivity of less than 1500 uS/m, which means that they are sensitive animals that will not suffer any damage if they consume this water. It was observed in the community of Malhadinha (Figures 14 and 15) that they were receiving water of 5500 uS/m, well above what is recommended.

Figure 14. Chicken sheds. Figure 15. Quail breeding sheds.

Goats and sheep can refuse water with high salt levels at first and then ingest water with higher levels, but with the risk of causing disease and even death. In order for the animals to adapt to the salinity of the water to be consumed, it is essential that it is supplied gradually, as a sudden change can cause greater damage to the intake of water and food and to the animal's health, causing excessive thirst, abdominal pain, vomiting, diarrhea and, in extreme cases, the animal may even die (ARAÙJO et al., 2011).

Due to the need to avoid any risk of economic losses, the National Academy of Sciences (1972) established that, from the point of view of the salinity of drinking water, animals consuming water with an electrical conductivity (EC) of less than 5 dS m^{-1} should be satisfied in almost all circumstances, which represents 31.40% of the water analyzed (1st collection) and 26.32% (2nd).

McGregor (2004) reports that, compared to drinking water, goats can accept brackish water up to 12.5 dS m^{-1}, which represents 90.70% (1^a collection) and 88.16% ($2^{(a)}$ collection) of the samples analyzed. These animals are able to adapt to drinking water with salinity levels of up to 9.5 dS m^{-1}, while maintaining their food intake; However, salinity levels higher than this result in a decline in food intake 79.07% of the samples are below 9.5 dS m^{-1} (1st collection) and 69.74% (2nd collection); in the Bravo site, goat farming was observed (Figure 16) with water of 6.42 dS m^{-1}.

Figure 16. Goat drinking high salinity water.

The CONAMA resolution (2005) classifies fresh waters as those with a salinity of 0.5 ppm or less, brackish waters with a salinity of more than 0.5 ppm and less than 30 ppm or saline waters with a salinity of 30 ppm or more. In view of the above, we can say that 100% of the samples are waters classified as saline.

Waters with electrical conductivity (salt content) ranging from 8.0 to 11.0 dS m^{-1} (5,120 and 7,040 mg L^{-1}), respectively, should be limited to ruminants, including goats and sheep. Waters with concentrations above 11.0 dS m^{-1} are considered high risk for young, pregnant and lactating animals.

(16.27% in the 1st collection) and 19.74% in the 2nd collection), while water with salt concentrations above 16.0 dS m^{-1} (10,240 mg L^{-1}) is not suitable for use by various animal species (RUNYAN and BADER 1994).

For dairy cattle 32.56% (1st collection) and 23.68% (2nd collection) of the samples are within the standard, for beef cattle 87.21% (1st collection) and 81.58% (2nd collection) of the samples are within the standard, for sheep and lambs 52.33% (1st collection) and 42,11% (2nd collection) of the samples are within the standard, for adult sheep 95.51% (1st collection) and 94.74% (2nd collection) of the samples are within the standard and for horses 18.60% (1st collection) and 15.79% (2nd collection) of the samples are within the permitted value for the chloride parameter.

With regard to chloride, 3.49% (1st collection) and 1.32% (2nd collection) of the samples are within the permitted value of 250 mg L^{-1} and 9.30% (1st collection) and 3.95% (2nd collection) of the samples are below 500 mg L^{-1}. Samples that are outside the standard can cause increased moisture in the excreta, especially in birds (MAM, 2014).

Excess chlorides in water intended for animal consumption can cause: Excessive thirst; Increased urinary excretion; Nasal discharge; Lack of appetite; Vomiting; Diarrhea; Abdominal pain; Behavioral symptoms; Prostration; Convulsions; Death (MAM, 2014).

For calcium, 91.86% (1st collection) and 89.47% (2nd collection) samples are below 500 mg L^{-1}. And only 7.41% (1st collection) and 10.53% (2nd collection) may present Functional disorders; Calcification of pipes and valves of supply equipment.

For the sodium parameter, 6.98% (Γ(,) collection) and 3.95% (2nd collection) samples were below 250 and 20.93% (1st collection) and 19.74% (2nd collection) samples were well below 500 mg L^{-1}.

With regard to potassium, both samples were below 250 and 500 mg L^{-1}. Values above the permitted level can cause an increase in the humidity of the excreta , especially in birds and other animal species.

According to Bagley et al. (1997), the criterion for using saline or brackish water for animal watering is that values of 1,000 ppm of total dissolved salts are considered low, making it possible to supply water to any animal species, which represents 5.81% (1[a] collection) and 0% (2[(a)] collection) of the water samples. On the other hand, concentrations of total dissolved salts in water ranging from 1,000 to 4,999 ppm are considered satisfactory for supplying sheep and cattle, but without harming their productive performance, they can cause temporary diarrhea or be poorly accepted by non-adapted animals, which accounted for 48.84% (1st collection) and 26.32% (2nd collection) of the samples analyzed. Between 5,000 and 6,999 ppm of total dissolved salts, the water can also be used for sheep and cattle, but its consumption by animals in advanced stages of pregnancy or lactation should be avoided, which represents

29.07% (1st collection) and 17.11% (2nd collection) of the samples analyzed.

From 7,000 to 10,000 ppm (13.95%) (1st collection) and 30.26% (2nd collection) of total dissolved salts, consumption should be avoided, but in exceptional situations this water can be fed to adult animals that are not under stressful conditions; however, it should not be fed to lactating animals, pregnant women, horses, sheep and young animals or those subject to high levels of heat stress or water loss. After these concentrations of salts in the water, it should not be fed to the animals.

Among the chemical elements, magnesium (Mg), when present in excess in water, can cause physiological disorders, especially in association with high salt concentrations (greater than 10.0 dS m^{-1} for sheep).

As for water consumption, Araùjo et al. (2011) reported that high concentrations of solids in water can affect its acceptability. This includes salt concentration. Lardy et al. (2008) state that increasing salt in the diet stimulates increased water consumption in all species due to the increased volume of urine required for salt excretion. Jaster et al. (1978) observed that lactating cows receiving drinking water or saline water (2500 ppm) had a significant difference in water consumption, with the animals receiving saline water consuming the most water (16.28°o) (Γ(1) collection) and 6.58% (2nd collection). These data are in line with those of Valtorta et al. (2008), who observed higher water consumption for lactating cows receiving water with 10,000 ppm salt (97.67%) (1st collection) and 73.68% (2nd).

It can be seen that the pH values of the water ranged from 6.1 to 10.1, most of which were within the limits allowed for class 3 brackish water by CONAMA Resolution No. 357/2005 and although we don't have a parameter for animals, we can correlate it with the tolerance limits for human consumption, which is between 6.0 and 9.5, according to Ordinance 2914/11 of the Ministry of Health, so it can be correlated that 95.35% in the 1st collection and 100% (2nd collection) are suitable for all animals.

3.6 THE MAGNESIUM CONTENT IN THE WATER

In 9.30% (Γ" collection) and 14.47% (2nd collection) of the water analyses, the magnesium value exceeded the limit of 41 meq L^{-1}, i.e. the highest value found was 66.92 meq L^{-1} (1st collection) and 57.62 meq $L^{(-1)}$ (2nd collection), not recommended for any type of animal, therefore for this parameter according to the limits established by the Australian Water Resources Council (1969), cited in Ayers and Westcot (1999). Therefore, this water cannot be offered to any animal, but it can be used as an augmentation to the best waters, through proportions and dilutions duly adjusted to the consumption limit of the animal category intended to use this water.

In the survey, 72.09% (1st collection) and 85.53% (2nd collection) were below 41 meq L^{-1}. This assessment follows the limits established by the Australian Water Resources Council (1969), cited in Ayers and Westcot (1999).

Thus, the Mg^2 content+ determined in the water must be taken into account, especially when the salinity exceeds 6.6 dS m^{-1} (4,000 mg $L^{(-1)}$) in water used by cattle and 10 dS m^{-1} (6,000 mg $L^{(-1)}$)) by sheep (Ayers and Westcot, 1994), which was the case when the water samples were above 6.6 (54.65%) and 10 dS m^{-1} (19.77%).

The values of magnesium salts present in the water represent another limitation of use, and for livestock activities, according to Figure 17, in the 1st [a] collection 54.65% of the samples have a magnesium concentration below 21 meq L^{-1} and in the 2nd collection 47.37%, i.e. they can be offered to confined poultry, pigs, horses, lactating cows, ewes and young lambs.

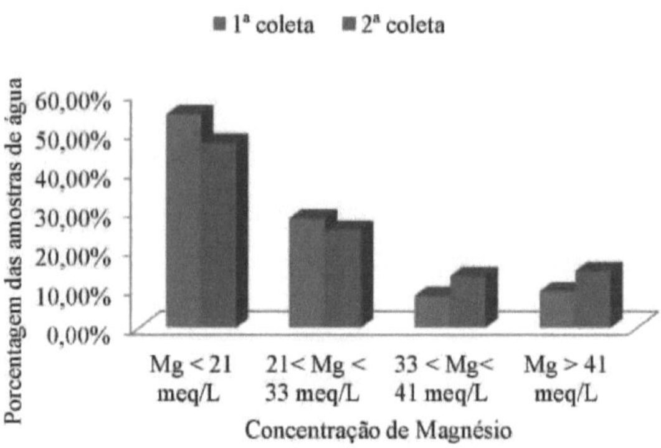

Figure 17. Magnesium content in water for animals

Of the 27.91% (1st collection) and 25% (2nd collection) of the samples analyzed with a magnesium concentration between 21 and 33 meq L^{-1}, this water can only be offered to adult beef cattle that are fed hay. A total of 8.14% (1st collection) and 13.16% (2nd collection) of the samples have a magnesium concentration between 33 and 41 meq L^{-1} and can only be offered to adult sheep that are fed hay. Therefore, for this parameter, the limits established by the Australian Water Resources Council (1969), cited in Ayers and Westcot (1999), are within the standard.

The animals that will consume these waters with high levels of magnesium need to be adapted to this diet, because animals that come from other places with low levels of salts can feel the toxicity even at lower levels. Variations in levels can change throughout the year, and in extreme cases of magnesium, the risk of it changing to higher values may not be perceived by the producer, and these sources require constant monitoring of chemical analysis.

3.7 CORRELATION BETWEEN WATER ELECTRICAL CONDUCTIVITY AND OTHER PARAMETERS

For the Pearson coefficient analyses, 86 water samples were used in the 1st [a] and 76 in the 2nd [a] collection and 78 that had the presence of sulphate (in both collections). The pH of the groundwater showed no tendency to vary in relation to the increase in electrical conductivity. The pH of the sources varied between 6.07 and 10.1, both independent of the degree of salinity. In this case, the variables are not correlated, i.e. the pH, according to Figure 18, shows a minimal positive correlation with the electrical conductivity of the water.

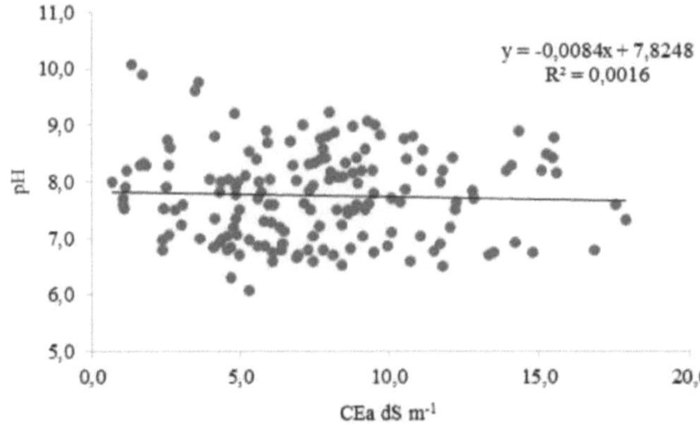

Figure 18. Correlation between pH values and water electrical conductivity

According to Figure 19, calcium shows up to 5 dS m^{-1}; a linear trend of calcium with electrical conductivity, above 5dS m^{-1} the trend is not linear having a correlation coefficient according to the Table of 0.61 showing moderate correlation with the electrical conductivity of the water.

The correlation is low and, for ECa greater than 10 dS m^{-1}, there is a greater dispersion between the points, reducing the correlation value.

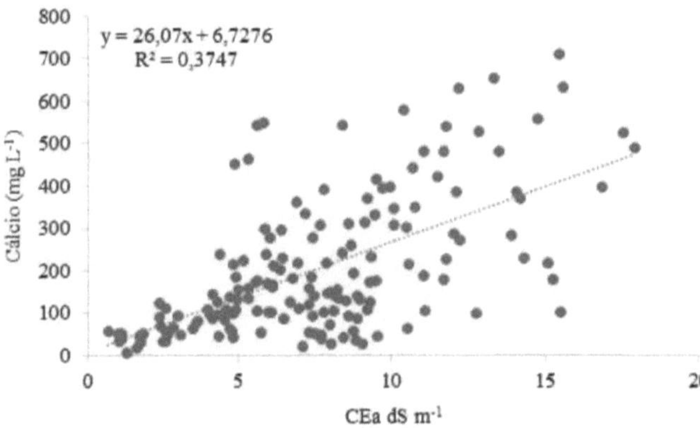

Figure 19. Correlation between calcium values and water electrical conductivity

According to Figure 20, magnesium has a linear trend in relation to electrical conductivity, with a correlation coefficient of 0.90, i.e. a strong correlation with the electrical conductivity of the water. The increase in magnesium values was directly proportional to the increase in electrical conductivity in underground sources. It can therefore be concluded that more than 80% of the variance in magnesium concentration is explained by the variation in ECa, with a strong positive correlation.

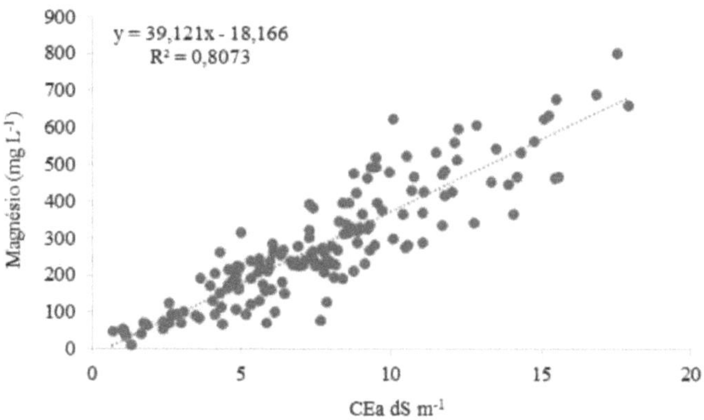

Figure 20. Correlation of magnesium values x electrical conductivity of water

It can therefore be concluded that more than 80% of the variance in magnesium concentration is explained by the variation in ECa, with a strong positive correlation. In the linear equation model obtained, the region's waters with values above 6.855 dS m^{-1} are very likely to have magnesium values above 250 mg/L, which for most animals is considered the limit level for animal watering, according to Ayres & Wescot (1999).

In groundwater, it was observed that up to ECa= 6.855 uS cm^{-1} , magnesium showed values below 250 mg L^{-1} (Figure 5), a range that is considered recommended for most animals (Ayers & Westcot (1999)). Westcot (1999), which justifies having equations of this nature to help the producer, when the information from the physical reading of the conductivity meter is a way of orienting the possible magnesium salt content in the *water*. This is important to avoid the risk of toxicity in animals, especially poultry (broilers), which is economically one of the most important rural activities in the municipality, according to Silva et al., 2016.

Assigning fictitious values of electrical conductivity to the equation, it was found that the safe limit for the use of water with magnesium contents below 250 mg L-1 (Ayers

& Westcot (1999) in groundwater is obtained when the water does not exceed values of ECa= 6,855 uS cm-1 without major risks for animal watering, and therefore surface water is identified as having a higher concentration of magnesium salts than groundwater. Lower concentrations of magnesium are observed in underground sources, because it is more soluble, magnesium is more difficult to precipitate because it is more stable in the face of chemical weathering, occurring in lower concentrations in underground sources (Shuqair, 2002).

Rocha (2008) found similar results in tube wells in the Rio do Peixe basin in Bahia, where electrical conductivity showed the highest positive correlation coefficient with sodium, followed by magnesium and calcium. Thus, the water in this study theoretically has a predominance of the salts sodium chloride (NaCl), calcium chloride ($CaCl_2$) and magnesium chloride ($MgCl_2$).

Sodium shows a linear trend with ECa, with a coefficient of 0.94 showing a strong correlation with the electrical conductivity of the water, even though there is a better straight line fit (Figure 21).

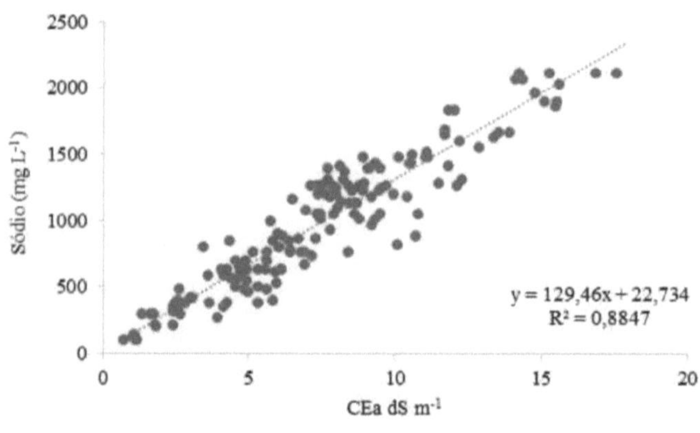

Figure 21. Correlation of sodium values x electrical conductivity of water

Potassium shows a linear trend up to 5 dS m^{-1}, with electrical conductivity; after this value there is a non-linearity, with a correlation coefficient of 0.46 showing a weak positive correlation with electrical conductivity (Figure 22). According to Rocha (2008), with regard to potassium ion, clay tends to fix it irreversibly, explaining the low levels of potassium ion in groundwater and the lack of correlation with electrical conductivity for the water studied.

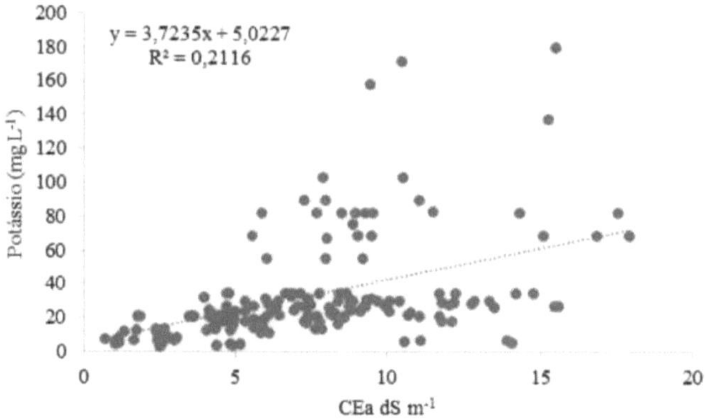

Figure 22. Correlation of potassium values x electrical conductivity of water

Carbonate shows little correlation with the electrical conductivity of the water, i.e. a weak positive correlation (Figure 23).

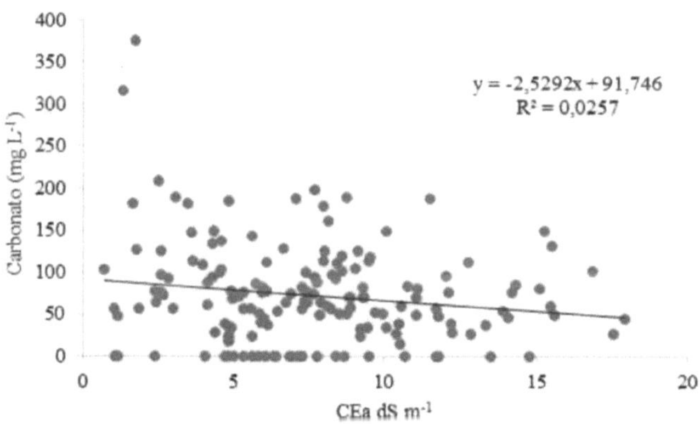

Figure 23. Correlation of carbonate values x electrical conductivity of water

Bicarbonate shows little correlation with the electrical conductivity of the water (Figure 24); therefore, the salinity of the waters in the crystalline region is not associated with variations in bicarbonate concentrations.

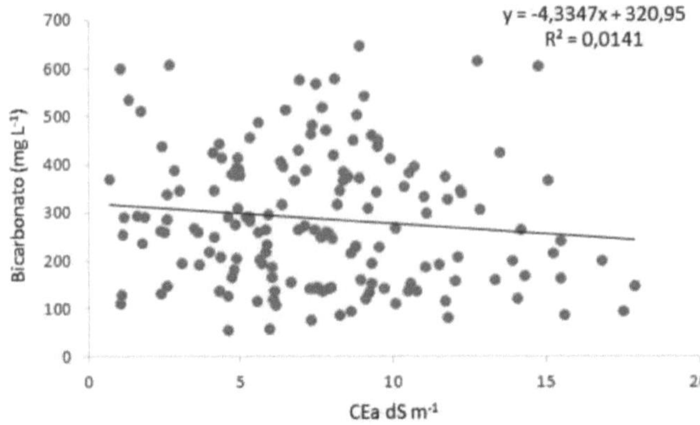

Figure 24. Correlation of bicarbonate values x electrical conductivity of water

Santos et al. (1984), working with groundwater from the crystalline region of Rio Grande do Norte, found that as electrical conductivity increased, sodium, calcium and magnesium grew in parallel, while bicarbonates fell very quickly.

Chloride shows a linear trend with electrical conductivity, with a correlation coefficient of 0.98, showing a strong correlation with the electrical conductivity of the water (Figure 25). The coefficients of determination and correlation were above 0.9 in all the analyses, allowing us to conclude that more than 90% of the variance in the concentration of this ion can be explained by the variation in ECa, i.e. there was a good fit between the analysis of the cation and the linear regression line, allowing us to develop a reliable equation for determining this ion from the value of electrical conductivity (ECa).

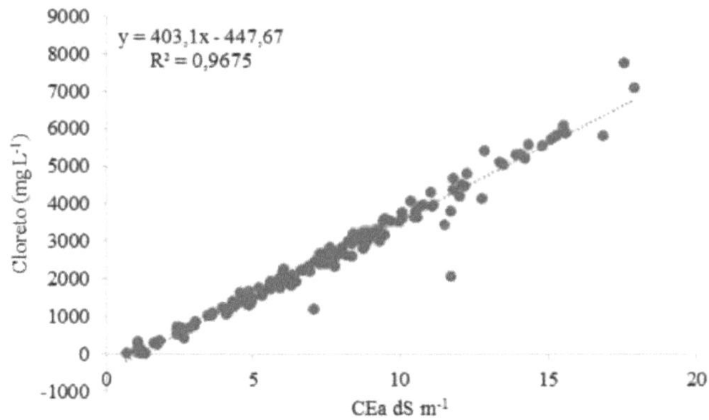

Figure 25. Correlation of chloride with the electrical conductivity of water

Filho et al. (2004) also found a strong correlation between chloride concentration and electrical conductivity in well and surface water samples in northern Ceara. Similar results were found by Maia, et al. (2012) in municipalities in northeastern Brazil.

Table 8 shows the individual equations for determining each of the salts from the value of the electrical conductivity of the source. The equation was determined by the linear trend line of the graphs, observing the coefficient of determination and the correlation coefficient of all the salts, in order to achieve the best fit of the samples to the linear regression line.

Table 8. Empirical equations, coefficient of determination and correlation coefficient between electrical conductivity (EC) and the main constituent salts of groundwater.

Results from Underground Sources			
Salts	**Groundwater source equations**	**Coefficient Determination (R^2)**	**ofCorrelation coefficient (R)**
Càlcio	Ca^{2+} = 26.07 CE + 6.7276	0,3747	0,6121
Magnesium	Mg^{2+} = 39.121 EC - 18.166	0,8073	0,8985
Sodium	At^{+} = 129.46CE + 22.734	0,8847	0,9406
Potassium	K^{+} = 3.7235 CE + 5.0227	0,2116	0,46
Chloride	Cl^{-}= 403.1 CE - 447.67	0,9675	0,9836

pH	pH = -0.0084CE+7.8248	0,0016	0,04
Carbonate	$CO_3^{=}$ = -2.5292CE+91.746	0,0257	0,1603
Bicarbonate	HCO_3^{-}= -4.3347CE+320.95	0,0141	0,1187

4. CONCLUSIONS

The water analyses carried out in the region showed a supply of inferior quality and high risk for poultry, which could induce the animal not to gain weight.

The pH, calcium, potassium, chloride and hardness values are above the maximum limit allowed for poultry. Combining the limitations of the chloride salt content with the total salt content of the water, chloride is the factor with the greatest impact on water quality, preventing it from being offered to the most sensitive animals, such as poultry.

The variables sodium, magnesium and chloride are the ones that best fit the straight line and have a strong positive correlation with the electrical conductivity of the water, which is explained by the equation. The equations generated are of great economic relevance to farming activities for rural producers and/or technical assistants, as they can use a portable conductivity meter to determine the electrical conductivity of the water and, using the equation, obtain an estimate of the sodium content, magnesium and chloride content at the source, allowing the water to be properly used for animal watering, avoiding water with very high salt levels that can cause diarrhea, poisoning, loss of weight gain, abortion in pregnant females or even the death of animals, with consequent financial losses and a reduction in the herd.

When wells with a high salt content are identified, it is recommended to use rainwater for dilution, allowing proper use and a greater volume of water available to serve the animals, i.e. water from the cistern and lower quality water from the tube well in the animal's drinking trough.

5. REFERENCES

AESA - Agência Executiva de Gestao das Aguas do Estado da Paraiba, accessed at < http://geo.aesa.pb.gov.br/ and http://www.aesa.pb.gov.br/ > in Sep 2016.

Good quality water: what is it? Avicultura Profesional, Athens, v. 6, n. 1, p. 14, 1988. BRAZIL. Ministry of Agriculture, Livestock and Supply. Available at: . Accessed on 05/05/20163.

AGRA, M. de F.; BARACHO, G. S.; BASiLIO, I. J. D.; NURIT, K.; COELHO, V. P.;

BARBOSA, D. de A. "Synopsis of the Medicinal Flora of Cariri Paraibano." Oecologia Brasiliensis. Electronic Journal. 11 (3): 323-330, 2007. Available at: <http://www.oecologia.biologia.ufrj.br>. Accessed on: 06 Nov. 2011.

ARAÙJO, G. G. L.; VOLTOLINI, T. V.; TURCO, S. H. N., Water in goat and sheep production systems. In: Goat and sheep production in the Semi-Arid. Petrolina, 2011, 553p.

AYERS, R. S.; WESTCOT, D. W. Water quality for agriculture. 3rd. ed. Rome: FAO, 1999 (FAO. Irrigation and Drainage Paper, 29).

BAGLEY, C. V.; AMACHER, J. K.; POE, K. F. Analysis of water quality for livestock. Logan: Utah State University, Cooperative Extension. 7p, 1997.

BLOCK SS. Disinfection sterilization and prevention, 4. ed. Philadelfia: Lea and Febiger, 1991. 1162p.

BRAZIL. Ministry of Health. Ordinance No. 2.914 of December 12, 2011. Provides for procedures to control and monitor the quality of water for human consumption and its standard of potability. Ministry of Health, **Official Gazette of the Union**, Brasilia, DF, Dec. 12, 2011.

BRAZIL. Ministry of Agriculture, Livestock and Supply. Available at: <www.agricultura.gov.br/animal/especies/aves >. Accessed on 05/05/2013.

CASTRO, E.S.O; JÛNIOR, B.T.B.R; PONTES, A.N; MORALES, G.P, Potability of Groundwater for Human Consumption in the Area of the Industrial Pole of Bacarena-

Parâ. Revista enciclopédia biosfera, Centro Cientifico Conhecer - Goiânia, v.10, n.19; p. 10, 2014.

CDRM Companhia de Desenvolvimento dos Recursos Minerais http://paraiba.pb.gov.br/cdrm-programa-perfuracao-de-900-pocos-artesianos-este-year/

CONAMA. Resolution No. 357 of 2005. Establishes the classification of fresh, brackish and saline waters in Brazil. Official Gazette of the Union. Brasilia, DF, 2005.

EMBRAPA - BRAZILIAN AGRICULTURAL RESEARCH Corporation. National Soil Research Center. Manual of soil analysis methods. 2ª ed. Rio de Janeiro, 2016. 212p

FALCÂO, E.C. Analysis of Risks to Environmental Degradation Using Spatial Multicriteria Evaluation in the Municipality of Boa Vista-PB. Master's degree dissertation. Federal University of Campina Grande. Campina Grande - Paraiba. 2013.

FAO (Rome, Italy). Estudios de caso de especies vegetales para zonas eridas y semieridas de Chile y Mexico. santiago: FAO regional office for Latin America and the Caribbean, 1996. 143p. il (FAO. Regional Office for Latin America and the Caribbean, Arid and Semi-arid Zones, 10).

FiGUEiREDO, R.M. Programa de reducao de patógenos. sao Paulo: Câmara Brasileira do Livro, p.81, 1999.

FILHO, O. A. S.; VERiSSIMO, L. S. SILVA, C. M. S. V.; SANTIAGO, M. M. F. Hydrochemical measurements of groundwater in the Irauçuba region, northern Cearà. XIII Brazilian Groundwater Congress, 2004.

http://www.cprm.gov.br/publique/media/medidas_hidroq.pdf 18 Oct. 2015.

FUNDAÇÂO INSTITUTO BRASILEIRO DE GEOGRAFIA E ESTATÌSTICA - IBGE. Accessed <http://www.ibge.gov.br/cidadesat/topwindow.htm?1> in Sep 2011.

BRAZILIAN INSTITUTE OF GEOGRAPHY AND STATISTICS - iBGE. Geography of Brazil. Northeast Region. Rio de Janeiro: SERGRAF, 1977. Available on CD.

BRAZILIAN INSTITUTE OF GEOGRAPHY AND STATISTICS - IBGE. Base maps of the municipalities of the state of Paraiba. Various scales. Unpublished.

GAMA, N.M.S.Q.; TOGASHI, C. K.; FERREIRA, N. T.; BUIM, M. R. ; GUASTALLI, E. L.; FIAGA, D. A. M. Technical Dissemination - Knowing the water used for poultry production. Arquivos do Instituto Biológico, Sao Paulo, v.70, n.1, p.43-49, jan./jun., 2008.

INGRACI C. et al. 1995 APINCO Conference on Poultry Science and Technology, p. 255-256, 1995.

JASTER, E. H.; SCHUH, J. D. E.; WEGNER, T. N. Physiological Effects of Saline Drinking Water on High Producing Dairy Cows. J. Dairy Sci. v.61, p.66- 71, 1978.

JENSEN, L. S.; MAURICE, D. V.; CHANG, C. H. Relationship of mineral content of drinking water to lever lipid accumulation in laying hens. Poultry Science, Champaign, v. 56, p. 260-266, 1977.

KRABBE, E; ROMANI, A . The importance of water quality and management in broiler production. XIV Brasil Sul Poultry Symposium and V Brasil Sul Poultry Fair - Chapecó, SC - Brazil, 2013.

LAGGER, J. R. et al. The importance of water quality in dairy production. Veterinaria Argentina, Buenos Aires, v.27, n.165, p.346-354, 2000.

LARDY, G., STOLTENOW, C., JOHNSON, R. Livestock and Water. North Dakota State University, Fargo, North Dakota. 2008.

LEESON, S. and J. D. SUMMERS. Commercial Poultry Nutrition. University Books. Guelph, Canada, p.350, 1997.

LEESON, S. and J. D. SUMMERS. Scott's Nutrition of the Chicken. University Books. Guelph, Canada, p. 591.

LIMA, G. J. M. M; PIOCZCOVSKI, G. D. Water: the main feed in animal production. Symposium on animal production and water resources, Concórdia, SC - Brazil, July , 2010.

LOGAN, J. Interpretation of chemical water analysis. Recife: US. Agency for International Development, 1965. 67 p.

MACARI, M. 1996. Water in industrial poultry farming. Jaboticabal. FUNEP. Brazil, p.128,1996.

MACARI M. and L. A. AMARAL. 1997. Importance of water quality and types of drinkers for broilers. In: Broiler Management Course. WPSA- BR. Brazil, p.168, 1997.

MACARI, M. 1996. Água na Avicultura Industrial, Jaboticabal: FUNEP, 128p, NRC - National Academy of Sciences. 1994. Nutrient Requirements of Poultry. National Academy Press. Washington, USA.

MACARI, M.; SOARES, N. M. Water in industrial poultry farming. Campinas: APINCO Foundation for Poultry Science and Technology, 2012. MACÊDO JAB, BARRA MM. Process of Disinfection with Organic Chlorinated Derivatives in Water for Public Supply. Hidro News, Supplement, year II, n.3, p.1-8, 2004.

MACÊDO JAB. Waters & waters. Belo Horizonte: CRQMG, p. 977, 2004.

MAIA, C. E. ; Rodrigues, K. K. P.; Lacerda, V. S. Relationship between bicarbonate and chloride in irrigation water. Irriga. Botucatu, Special Edition, p. 206 - 219, 2012.

MARKS, H. L. 1987. Poultry Science. 66:1895.

McGREGOR, B. A. Water quality and provision for goats. Australian Government. Rural Industries Research and Development Corporation, p. 19. 2004.

MMA-MINISTÉRIO DO MEIO AMBIENTE; SRH-SECRETARIA DE RECURSOS HiDRICOS. PNRH-National Water Resources Plan: executive summary. Brasilia, ISBN 85-7738-013-0, 2006. 135p.

MOLLE, F and CADIER, E. Manual do Pequeno Açude. SUDENE/ORSTOM/TAPI, 1992. 523p

MOUCHREK, E. Water quality. Revista AVIMIG, Belo Horizonte, v.4, n. 34, p. 14-15, 2003.

NASCIMENTO, M, do S. B.; OLIVEIRA, M. E. Diversity and use of native plants.

Technical article. 2005. Available at: Accessed on: 06 nov. 2011.

NATIONAL RESEARCH COUNCIL. Nutrients and toxic substances in water for livestock and poultry. Washington, DC. National Academy of Sciences. 1974.

NERI LC, HEVITTI D, SCHREIBER GB. Can epidemiology elucidate the water history? American Journal of Epidemiology, v. 99, p.75-88, 1975.

OLIVEIRA, M.V.A.M. Water resources and animal production - legislation and aspects

general. Symposium on Animal Production and Water Resources, Concórdia, Sc - Brazil, 2010.

PALHARES, J. C.P. Environmental impact in broiler production - a review of the Brazilian scenario. In: Environmental Management in Poultry Farming. Available at: cnpsa.embrapa.br/sgc/sgc_publicacoes/publicacao_s3v74t2l.pdf. Accessed on

09/05/2013. EMBRAPA. Document series, p. 149, 2011.

PARAIBA. Government of the State of Paraiba. Planning Secretariat. State Plan and Water Resources Management System. Hydrogeological Characterization of the State of Paraiba. Annex 2. Campina Grande: SEPLAN/ATECEL, 1994. LSPP. (Agreement FDE-028/93).

PENDLETON, E.W, SCHEIDELER, S.E. Water quality basics for the poultry producer. Poultry Digest, Mt. Morris, v. 54, n. 1, p. 10-14, 1995. POMIANO JD.

Water management as a nutrient. Lima: _____ p. 1-31, 2002. PESTI, G.M., S.V.

AMATO AND L.R. MINEAR. 1985. Poultry Science. 64:803-808. Van Gulic, P. J. M. M. 2003. Iron in the ground water. Internet - ProviNet. http://nftalliance.com.br/artigos/ebooks/a-importancia-da-agua-na-avicultura
MARKS, H. L. 1987. Poultry Science. 66:1895.

PENZ, M.A. The importance of water as a nutrient in broiler production. Federal University of Rio Grande do Sul, 2002. Available at VIOLA, E. S.; VIOLA, T. H.; LIMA, G. J.M.M; AVILA, V. S. Agua na avicultura: importância, qualidade e exigências. In: Environmental Management in Poultry Farming. Available at: cnpsa.embrapa.br/sgc/sgc_publicacoes/publicacao_s3v74t2l.pdf. Accessed on 10/03/2016. EMBRAPA. Document series, p. 149, 2011.

PNRH - PLANO NACIONAL DE RECURSOS HiDRICOS. 2006. Panorama and the State of Brazil's Water Resources - volume 1. Ministry of the Environment. Brasilia.

POMIANO JD. Water management as a nutrient. Lima: ___ p. 1-31, 2002.

ROCHA, T. S.; Dissertation: Evaluation of the Quality of Water from Tubular Wells in the Rio do Peixe Basin Equipped with Desalinators, with a View to the Economic Use of Tailings Salts, Salvador 2008.

RUNYAN, C.; BADER, J. Water quality for livestock and poultry. In: AYERS, R. S.; WESTCOT, D. W. Water quality for agriculture. Rome: FAO, 1976. 1994 (FAO. Irrigation and Drainage Paper, 29).

SANTOS, J. P., AZEVEDO, S. G.; MISTRETTA, G. Novos aspectos da salinizaçao das águas subterrâneas do cristalino do Rio Grande do Norte. Sao Paulo, SP: IPT, 1984.27p. (Technical communication, 314).

SAWYER, C.; MCCARTY, P. L. Chemistry for environmental engineering. NewYork: McGraw-Hill Book Company, 1987. 532 p.

SHUQAIR, S. M. S. Thesis presented as part of the requirements for obtaining the Degree of Doctor of Science in the Area of Nuclear Technology-Materials. Study of the contamination of soil and groundwater by toxic elements originating from the tailings of the figueira coal mines in the state of Paranâ. IPEN - Nuclear and Energy Research Institute. Autarchy associated with the University of São Paulo 2002.

SOARES, N. M. Water quantity and quality in poultry production. Symposium on animal production and water resources, Concórdia, SC - Brazil, July 2010.

VALTORTA, S. E.; GALHARDO, M. R. A.; GREGORTE, R. F. Effect of salinity on water consumption of Iecheras cows in lactation during dry periods. In: 28th Argentine Congress of Animal Production. Bahia Blanca- Argentina, 2005.

VIOLA, E. S; VIOLA T. H.; LIMA, G. J. M. M. DE; AVILA, V. S. de. Water in poultry farming: importance, quality and requirements. In: EMBRAPA, 2011. Environmental Management in Poultry Farming. Documents 149. Concórdia, Embrapa, p. 37-123, 2011.

VOHRA N P. Water quality for poultry use. Feedstuffs, Minnetonka, v. 7, p.24-25, 1980.

WORLD HEALTH ORGANIZATION. Guidelines for drinking water quality. 2. ed. Geneva: WHO, v.1,1999.

WILLADINO, L.; CAMARA, T.R. Physiological aspects of salt stress in plants. In: NOGUEIRA, R. J. M. C.; ARAÙJO, E. L.; WILLADINO, L. Estresses ambientais: danos e beneficios em plantas. Recife, 2005. p. 118-126

MIX
Papier aus verantwortungsvollen Quellen
Paper from responsible sources
FSC® C105338

Printed by Books on Demand GmbH, Norderstedt / Germany